Managing Morale, And Motivating People

2nd Edition

By Nick Sharrer, CPA, CMA, CFM

Table of Contents

Why Morale is Important

Everyone wants to work in an environment where they enjoy coming to work. When you enjoy coming to work, it's usually because something about it makes you feel good about yourself. And when working makes you feel good about yourself, you won't necessarily mind working more. If, on the other hand, coming into work does not make you feel good about yourself, you may start worrying about it the night before. You won't want to get there any earlier than you have to, or stay longer, and you won't feel that there is any reason to do more than the minimum.

It's not hard to see why companies and teams with high morale easily produce more per employee, all else being equal, and do not have as high of turnover as other companies. Turnover costs are quite high; you have to pay to advertise, take the time to interview, possibly pay commissions to recruiters, and you have to retrain the new hire for your company's needs.

There often exists a disconnect between what managers think employees value, and what employees actually value. It's common for managers to believe that an employee values salary and extrinsic rewards more than appreciation and intrinsic rewards, but studies have shown that employees value intrinsic rewards, and a lack of personal stress at work, far more than they value pay or extrinsic rewards.

Consider it this way, if you were paid 10% more to work somewhere where your boss was going to yell at you every day, call you things that were inappropriate, and embarrass you in front of your co-workers and friends, I doubt that many people would jump at the opportunity to take that job if they already had a job where morale was high, and they felt good about themselves when they came into work, even if the pay was slightly less.

You will reduce the cost of turnover if you can maintain high morale in the workplace! Since people now expect to enjoy their jobs, or at least not mind coming into work, if you can maintain high morale you will have long-term employees. You can avoid costly advertising for new employees, costly mistakes made by new employees who need to be trained, or the loss of productivity from the person who trains them to prevent those mistakes. In many professions, it can take several months to a year for a person to fully understand the ins and outs of their job and to reach their full potential. If you have more complicated or manual systems, it will usually take longer. How can you afford not to keep morale high?

The Ego

Sigmund Freud described the Ego, the Super Ego, and the Id. I'm going to go one step further, I'm sure many psychology majors, including my wife, will say you can't do that. But I'm going to say they're all really related to the same thing. What I'm referring to is the sense of one's self as a human being.

The "Ego" is the sense of self in terms of needing to believe that we are valuable. It's our need to feel good about ourselves. If you watch small children, it's not hard to understand why we're born wanting to be "the best" at something. It's up to parents and guardians to teach these new human beings manners so that they can function with others in the world and become able to coexist without the world revolving around them. But does a part of this ever completely go away? Is there not an adult out there who would not want to be the best looking person, or the smartest? Is this not a part of what drives us to act?

The "Super Ego" was supposed to be what most people call the conscience. But to believe that you are good simply because you are good to others is still done to believe that you are good, and the need to believe that you are good is the "Ego." So here's why I'm saying they're really the same.

The "Id" has to do with desire, and is often attributed to someone's sex drive. But do we not do things because those things, in some way, make us feel good about ourselves? If a child plays games, do they not want to win? If someone playing a game with people they respect loses on purpose, is it not because they want the other people to like them? Or that bringing joy to those they are interacting with makes them feel that they are a good person, which makes them feel that they are good?

When someone's sex drive inspires them to obtain the affections of another, they want that person to love them, and to feel that they are good. As humans, we want to be loved in return. When someone doesn't return our affection, especially in youth, it's common to want them even more. We often find ourselves wanting someone mainly because we can't have them. If we were to win them, their affection would be an ultimate prize; it would make us feel worth more than we felt during the time when the person did not believe us to be their equal, or to be their personal desire. We want to be desired because it makes us feel that we are good.

When we parent children, they contain half of our DNA; they're an extension of our own lives and our material. A parent saving their child from danger is also saving a part of themselves, because their children are a part of them. They're the part that we fully expect to continue after our own bodies have died.

Long after we have died, and long after anyone can even remember us, if our children's children continue to procreate, then our genes will still continue to exist in the DNA of living humans many years after our own bodies have expired.

Not everyone decides that becoming a parent is the best for their survival, because some people choose to leave behind ideas or their work instead. What I'm merely pointing out is that this human trait has been born into us through evolution. This want to feel good about one's self is congruent with the want to survive or for something that we value to survive.

Every person wants to believe that their life is worth-while. That they are good at something or that they are of value, that they're important. This doesn't mean that they have to value their own life. Many people have given their own lives for causes they believed in because they believed those causes to be their mission, their purpose in life . . . to be more important than their own existence. They could value themselves for the good that they believe they provide for their children, or their church, or their community, their friends, you name it. It's different for every person, but every person has something that they believe to be worth more than just mere breathing and existence.

Some might say that this is all selfish, but is evolution not selfish? Those who believe themselves to be worthy of life, and to believe that their genes are worth passing on have continued to exist in the form of future generations while those who do not share these views soon take themselves out of the gene pool.

To feel good about oneself is to believe that you are worthy of existence. And although not everyone who feels great about themselves and feels worthy of existence goes on to procreate, they are more likely to do so. If we didn't want to be alive, we would simply choose to not be.

Some might try to tie this into the meaning of life, a whole separate topic, but for our purposes all we need to know is how this is going to affect what we want – to manage morale.

The lesson from this chapter is that every person has an evolutionary need to feel good about themselves and to truly believe that they are worthy to exist. Your actions and communications with them will either convince them that you also believe them to be good and worthy of existence, or that you do not care about their existence. If your communications with them confirm their sense of self, they will feel positively about what you have said.

If your communications, through both actions and words, contradict their belief that they are good, they will perceive your actions as negative.

The more you confirm their beliefs, the more they will call your very company positive and desirable. The more you contradict their beliefs, the more the opposite will be true.

Intrinsic Rewards

Intrinsic rewards are those that we feel internally and are not entirely related to the gain of possessions. Charity is usually done because a person giving their time to a cause gains a feeling of self worth. Doing good for others, and seeing that they have been able to breathe easier because of your influence can give you the feeling of having done something worthwhile, selfless, and kind. You gain, in return, the feeling that you are a kind person. Being kind is generally thought to be good, and in return, you feel good about yourself.

People are usually appreciative of someone who is kind, or someone who has done more than is expected, and when this appreciation is communicated and felt internally, it becomes a reward.

While watching a circus act, I once observed an elephant who was being rewarded for tricks with peanuts by its trainer. Someone in the crowd spoke out: "Look, he works for peanuts." Now, a peanut doesn't offer much in the way of nutrition to an animal the size of an elephant, so then why did the elephant consider a peanut to be something of value for putting its feet up and performing tricks? . . . because the peanut had become an intrinsic reward.

The peanut was in no way going to offset the number of calories that the elephant had used in performing those tricks, but by offering the token peanut for each trick performed, the elephant felt appreciated, it was actually an intrinsic reward and a very effective one in this case.

Now salary is usually an extrinsic reward, and we'll get to that in the next chapter, but when it comes to compensation there are several intrinsic factors. If you give someone a bonus for a job well done, and communicate that it's because of a job well done, that makes them feel good about themselves. It's telling them, "I appreciate you and your efforts so much that we're allotting a reward to let you know that we value what you've done and what you regularly do. We value you as an employee and as a person."

In terms of regular compensation, it's easy to believe

yourself to be more valuable when you believe that you're being paid well because your abilities and skills are valued by someone so highly that they're willing to pay higher than the average in the market or in the company, or in the job pool in general, just to get your services. This makes you feel valued, and that makes you feel good about yourself. People often gauge their success on their salary, and believe that this translates into social strata; this, in effect, is an intrinsic reward.

The biggest intrinsic reward that I have ever seen is that which we call love. When we desire someone's affection, when we believe that person to be a catch, and we find ourselves valuing their attention more than any other, there is no greater reward than to receive their affection and attention in return. If we actually receive love in return from those whom we ourselves love, then there can be no greater intrinsic reward felt, at least in my book. Now love isn't something that is common in the workplace, so let's focus on mutual respect. But I hope you will see my point.

To further understand this underlying reaction, the human body has several hormones and chemicals that promote a sense of well-being, happiness, interest, or even anxiety and depression. When you do something or are participating in something that interests you, it actually has a chemical affect on your brain, primarily it causes an increase of dopamine, which stimulates a sense of wellbeing and a sense of happiness. Drug users, who use substances such as cocaine or stimulant-effect drugs, often get a rush of dopamine, and it's that feeling that causes many of them to engage in this kind of behavior.

The negative side is, overly artificial levels of this chemical can cause all kinds of side effects, including hallucinations and the perceptions of both sights and sounds that are not really there. This is further correlated with true schizophrenia where extremely high levels of dopamine have been found in patients.

So not only do intrinsic rewards make us feel good in general, they actually have a positive effect on the chemicals in the brain. Is it any wonder that people will seek and respond well to intrinsic rewards? The easiest way to offer an intrinsic reward is with sincere, honest, open, and sometimes public, appreciation.

Extrinsic Rewards

Extrinsic rewards are usually physical, such as salary, bonuses, and benefits. These are basic things that people need to live, and they work for to support themselves and their families.

Compensation should be competitive, you don't want to lose your key positive people to a competitor because you aren't offering them as much as they could be making elsewhere. Although we'd like to think that people work for us simply because they enjoy spending time with us, they have needs and wants outside of work, and their work is their means to afford these things.

Compensation also needs to be perceived as fair, or it can affect the ego and the intrinsic rewards mentioned earlier.

People who are experiencing financial hardship and who are forced to deal with worry over their lower order needs, compared to the more discretionary needs, are going to face challenges in finding motivation at work. It's much easier to focus on solving the problems of others if your own needs are being met.

In an extreme example, if you're starving for food, you probably don't care too much about whether or not your employer is able to save money or produce items faster as long as you're still able to get what you're currently making.

But on the other hand, if your own needs are met, you have clothing, food, shelter, and enough change left over to blow off some steam sometimes on some impulse items, then it's going to be easier for you to care if your employer can produce more or deliver goods or services faster. In the latter case productivity could potentially become an interesting challenge like a puzzle that's at least entertaining, if nothing else.

Something that many companies have tried in the past is to freeze salaries. In an attempt to maintain costs, it's easy to say that no one gets a raise, and that way you don't have to evaluate who would get a raise, or deal with the feelings of unfairness when some get raises and some don't. But what usually happens is that the most marketable people are still worth something to your competitor. And if market wages are rising and inflation is cutting into your employees' earning power, they're going to consider looking around if their needs and wants could be better fulfilled by working for your competitor.

People's personal needs and wants are often far stronger outside of work. They could be supporting a family, buying a house, getting ready to send kids to college, getting ready to replace an old car, saving for retirement, or something else that's important to them. If you stop comparing what you're paying your top performers to the amount they could be making while working for your competition, you could very well find yourself being left with only the poor performers who couldn't get a job somewhere else while the top performers have moved on. In this case, you must offer them something intrinsic that other competing employers aren't offering, and also be sure to pay them well.

The Mission

The mission at hand is to foster high morale. And by fostering high morale, I'm talking about aligning the team's mission with the missions of its members. Every person has a career mission, a personal mission, and a general mission that their lives are headed towards. They may not be able to vocalize what their mission in life is, or what they personally want to get out of life, but something about the operations of the team should align with their own personal values and mission.

During times of war, soldiers who believe in what they are fighting for can do some of the most amazing things. Soldiers who do not personally believe in the cause will be likely to desert or hide for cover longer and not be willing to put forth any risks on their own part that they do not have to in order to simply stay alive . . . because their mission has turned into staying alive long enough to get through it and get back to what they believe is important.

During the French and Indian wars in the early 1700s, England and its colonial soldiers had many things to write home about in regards to the adversaries they were confronted with. On one hand, the Native Americans would fight fiercely, and if they ran out of arrows they were just as likely to engage in combat by hand using knives at close range. If they caught a colonial or English soldier, they might even scalp him or set him on fire. One of my own ancestors was captured during these wars and was set on fire as a personal punishment during warfare.

So why would these warriors go to such extreme measures and

take the battles so personally? . . . because they were fighting for their home and their way of life. They knew that if the English won, their homeland would be taken away and their way of life would end. For them, this fighting was directly in line with their mission.

During those same wars, the French soldiers stationed in the Northern part of the continent would use cannon fire from within forts, and they would fire muskets from a distance. But when confronted at a close distance, they would drop their weapons and surrender. The English accounts described this behavior as being quite the opposite of the native adversaries in the same wars. Now, the majority of the French military forces stationed in the Americas who were not officers were recruited former prisoners. That's right! They had formerly been confined to a French prison cell, staring at disease and sharing space with rats until they were given the option of leaving that cell if they agreed to serve in the military overseas. This must have seemed like a more attractive option at the time. At least a person could get out in the fresh air again, and many of them were predicting that no conflict would occur, but that the assignment would be merely a threat to deter an invasion. They weren't serving because of any aligned mission with their country's colonial interests; they were simply trying to escape a continued prison fate.

It's no wonder then that when confronted with the risk of

death, they were not interested in giving their lives for a country far away that had once imprisoned them. This was certainly not in line with their personal missions.

So what is the personal mission of each person on your team? What do they want from work, and what do they believe in? What are their values, and how do they want to be perceived by others? A person can hardly contain who they are; we're naturally social creatures and when asked enough about ourselves, we'll tell our own stories. Each personal story that someone tells you reveals a little about them and about who they are. Pay attention and find out what they want specifically, then see if you can give that to them.

There are several things that most people want and expect from the workplace: clear communication about what's expected of them and what they are expected to perform; how they are going to be evaluated; a lack of negativity; the existence of a family atmosphere where they can feel comfortable and respected; some social needs through working and communicating with others whom they perceive as their friends at work, and even praise.

Give people more of what they enjoy doing. Each person will enjoy certain tasks more than others, and this is usually because something about the task makes them feel good about themselves. Find out what each person's strengths are and give them more duties to display to those strengths.

It's natural for people to enjoy the tasks that they're good at because once again it makes them feel good about themselves. If someone is analytical, give them more analytical and detailed projects. If someone is more people-oriented, give them opportunities to build relationships for your team and to answer questions or be the spokesperson for meetings, if needed. If someone loves to write, put them in charge of your written narratives.

In my own experience, I had always wanted to be a financial controller. During my days in college my interests consistently fell towards the use of numbers to analyze economics and to solve economic problems, while at the same time being able to view a picture of how a business was doing and how different strategies had really affected results. These skills became my strengths, and I loved every opportunity I was given to use them.

I was given the opportunity to become a controller much earlier than I anticipated. I knew that a position was open for a subsidiary controller role, and I thought that it would be one of the most exciting roles within the company. Better yet, it was for the Canada operations where my mother's family is from, so I had an even greater personal interest. I expressed my interest, although I had fewer total years in the field than the position was being advertised for, and I asked what I should do in the mean time to prepare for when something like that might open up again.

To my amazement, Kristen, my boss, considered me for the job. She considered what I had done during my career and during my time on her team, and I was completely surprised when she offered me the position itself even though I had fewer years out of school than the advertisement asked for. Not only that, but she was one of the best managers and mentors a person could ask for, and through that relationship there wasn't anything I wouldn't do for her. She had a way about her that made people feel good about themselves. She laughed a lot, she knew everyone personally, and she honestly expressed appreciation for work once it was performed.

After the initial training, I found my ideas and my performance to get better and better every year to the point where I was leading projects I had only heard of in my former role. I was interested in the position itself and that interest translated into some of the best evaluations I had ever had. But most importantly, I enjoyed the job! And I especially enjoyed working for her. My morale while working for her was the highest I had ever experienced and I literally couldn't wait to arrive at work each day because there was something of a personal value that I derived from it, and the fact that she gave me the chance to become what I wanted to be.

When someone shows interests in the skills of another, it's quite a compliment to the person whose skills are being recognized and applied. If you can find the most productive setting for each team member, you should be in line with their own missions. And when you're in line with their personal missions you'll find some of the greatest morale and loyalty.

Create a Positive

Culture

If you can create a positive culture
where people actually look forward
to coming in to the workplace, you

will certainly be on your way to having high morale.

Everyone wants to work in an environment where they feel appreciated. The value of sincere honest appreciation cannot be underestimated. This needs to be personal, and it needs to confirm the person's own sense of ego in such a way that they truly and honestly believe the appreciation they are given. And to do this, you really must mean it. If you are false in your praise, or feign compliments, people will see right through you and it won't have the effect that you desire. Everyone has something they do well, even if it's expected of their position. Find out what they're doing well and thank them personally for it. Everyone likes to hear good things about themselves.

It's also extremely effective if you can foster an environment where people offer praise of each other. Receiving a compliment from a co-worker about something you've done can often be valued by the person even more than praise given by an authority figure, because to earn praise from your peer means that what you did must have gone above and beyond what is just seen as a requirement that you perform for your management. It means that what you did was so great that others took note of it and said something. It can also show that these people are less in competition with each other and are more concentrated on working as a highly-effective team where all members' contributions are seen as worthy and important, and people are not needing to compete with each other at a fierce level for that desired promotion or raise or to stay employed during anticipated future layoffs. This is congruent with the idea of an island society where food and resources are plentiful and no one has to fight for survival because there's plenty of everything to go around.

If resources are seen as extremely scarce (think of praise as a resource), then humans and animals will compete to the death to obtain those resources. If only a few can survive, then it's evolutionary nature to want to be one of those few; and then it becomes about not how great you are, but about how much better you are. If the general feeling is that you need to be better than everyone else in order to survive, then that warm and friendly feeling that people can provide for one another goes away. But if everyone feels that they will get what they want and need while others can do the same, then there's no need to feel so competitive. And without a highly internally competitive culture, there won't be a need for jealousy.

Making Work Fun

Not everyone at first is under the impression that work can be fun. We're often faced with criticism, having to admit one's own mistakes, dealing with the complaints of a customer on the phone, or even feeling the fringes of a co-worker who's having a bad day. But believe it or not, you can actually play at work in such a way that you're still just as productive.

When we're children, life is all about play; we play games, we act our part. Little girls will often play with dolls, boys will often play with trucks or pretend to be firemen or cops and robbers or pretend to be whatever they want to be that day. So much of this is actually preparing for the real world and acting out what it would be like. It's like trying on new hats, and to them it's play. It's fun! So then why do so many adults complain that their actual work lives are a burden, something painful to be endured, perhaps even a sacrifice?

For many it's because what they are doing is not at all to them like the feeling they once had when they were young and were playing. What is our daily life really? How different is playing football from performing physical work? How is working different than when we were young and were playing computer games?

If you have physical work, turn it into a sport. Make that task into the next great football play and get your co-workers in on it, too. Remember to be able to laugh at yourselves, you need to be able to feel like you can joke lightly and laugh. When you were playing, did you laugh when you fell if you weren't hurt? . . . Or did you cry or complain when it didn't hurt? Tackle football is a painful sport; I'm not volunteering for it myself at my age. But when I was young, my neighborhood friends and I would go to the local park and play football. We got muddy, we got dirty, we got tired . . . and we had one heck of a good time!

The elements in play involve individuals, such as making a game out of how many palettes can I move today like Packman going through the maze absorbing the little golden points. Or it can be made even better by getting the whole team involved. When you feel comfortable and safe enough to play and involve your co-workers in an appropriate attitude, like the one you would involve during play, you can make almost anything fun. If you deal with a computer for most of the day, treat it like a giant puzzle, or one of the strategy video games that so many children play today that they would gladly skip their homework for another hour of it if they could . . . because having fun is all in our outlook, your attitude, and in the morale and comfort level of the people around you.

If a co-worker isn't able to laugh and smile with the team, and insists that everything be as serious as a funeral home, well that's not going to make things very fun. Some people don't naturally play well with others, and people are hard to change, but even the least sociable people will often give in, have fun, and forget their worries if they feel included.   If you don't feel included yourself, why? You deserve to be here as much as anyone, and if someone else is feeling the same, you can remind them of that too. It doesn't matter where we were born, or what social group we belong to, black, brown, or white, male or female, we can still be brothers in the family at work!

Productivity can be contagious if it's allowed to be fun. I'm not suggesting that the fun needs to be outside of the working tasks. I'm actually advocating that the work itself can be turned into a sport or a game among the team members, and that the social interaction and camaraderie can be just what was needed to bring the team together and make everyone feel like they belong.

Everyone wants to feel like they belong, it makes us feel good about ourselves; our friends are those who make us feel the best because then we know we're not alone in the world. We want others to value our company, and the first way to start is to value the company of others . . . and the quickest way to make friends is to find a way to play together.

The Belief of
Fairness

When people believe that things are fair, and that people are true with them, they will believe that politics or unfair obstacles won't prevent them from completing their own personal missions.

Office politics often become the source for feelings of unfairness. When it's perceived that someone is thought higher of by management because they've done something that made the boss feel good about themselves, this can be seen as favoritism or brown-nosing by others. Generally this comes down to feelings that decisions being made are not fair and are being made on superficial or less than accurate information.

Some people may have been more worthy of certain favors or

promotions, but they bragged about their accomplishments less and their work was not recognized. People often have a tendency to hire their friends or to hire those who speak more than others, or they may treat people differently based on looks or general popularity.

It isn't really any different than the politics for presidential or government positions. Popularity doesn't always correlate with skills or abilities, and when people believe that political factors have caused them to be treated unfairly, or that they will be treated unfairly due to these types of factors, their morale lowers.

During my time in college, I witnessed something that surprised me. I was an academic and I qualified for the accounting honors society, which I considered to be quite an honor. I made many friends through the organization and every week I would look forward to a different event or a speaker to educate us about the field. Due to low enrollment at the college, the regular accounting society (the club that would let people join who didn't have the grades to qualify for the honors society) shared the same meeting times as the honors society. Although some recruiters would directly ask when speaking with a student if they were in the honors society or the lower requirement club as a way to filter a person's technical performance, many recruiters couldn't tell the difference because we were all in the same room, until they read the student's resume.

I thought that members of the honor society would find jobs first, and most did, but my surprise came when officers of the lower requirement club, who didn't have high grades, were often chosen for positions with firms before the honors students who were less involved politically, or who had run for an office but had lost the election.

I figured that many of these officers were being chosen for their public speaking skills, or their future ability to make sales, but I was surprised again when I learned that some of them were actually quite disorganized and didn't necessarily possess the traits that someone would expect of an accountant.

One woman named Mary actually failed two accounting courses, but she was somewhat pretty at the time, and had won the election mainly because she was quite popular and the boys in the class enjoyed talking to her. Even though she wasn't showing promise as a future accountant, she was hired by a prestigious firm before most of the honors students.

Although surprised to hear of the results, I once again figured that it would be for her future salesmanship, or other technical abilities that she would be able to provide to the firm. Many years later after my own public accounting career, I worked alongside someone who had been a manager at that firm. I learned through him that her lack of technical abilities actually wound up costing the firm money in rework, and that her looks were only skin deep as she would get into heated arguments with the clients, and after only six months, she was let go.

I later learned that she became a wine tasting clerk, which doesn't require a degree in accounting to perform. But I did take note that many members of the honors society many years ago felt that the hiring decision was entirely political, and after learning what happened, I've remembered it as an example of politics influencing a decision that was seen as unfair by some of the less physically attractive people who would have loved to have that job with the prestigious firm.

Wherever there are people, there will be politics; it's just that some places are better than others. Try to keep the politics in your organization from becoming so strong that decisions are viewed as unfair.

Exclusionary social circles (or cliques) are another area where things might appear to be unfair. As social creatures, we like to be surrounded by our friends; our friends make us feel good about ourselves, and that makes us feel happy to come into work. But when these friendships begin to influence business decisions without business merit, they can create barriers for those who may have less in common personally with the people holding the power to make decisions.

If a portion of the office plays golf on a regular basis, it's tempting to talk business while on the golf course, even if it's with friends you've made through work. But it's also very easy for business decisions to actually be made on the golf course itself. Now, those who aren't good at golf or who never learned to play may be inadvertently excluded from these decisions. They may return from their weekend to find that decisions have been made in favor of those who were on the golf course that weekend, and they may feel unfairly excluded.

Let's say, for example, that the boss goes golfing with two subordinates from work and one of the subordinates, in particular, is a great golfer. It's hard not to be impressed by another's skill even if it isn't related to work. And let's say that the other golfer is a good golfer, but more than anything is great at telling jokes and keeps everyone in a good mood during their weekend excursion.

Now let's say that the boss has two middle manager positions to fill, but has four eligible workers to consider for the open positions. It can be quite tempting to want to give those two friends the manager positions. You know them; you like to be around them, and one of them shows confidence in a game that makes them seem like a confident person. But will that be fair to the other candidates who may have worked just as hard or even harder, and may have some very impressive business skills and be great with people . . . but they just weren't able to play golf with you?

Another common perception of unfairness is the difference between morning people and night people. My first example comes during my time in public accounting when some people would get there at eight a.m. and some would get there at nine. On one occasion during a busy season I overheard two people who arrived at nine in the morning and were planning to leave at nine in the evening say, "we're working harder than those people who left an hour ago; we should be getting paid more than they are."

But the thing they didn't realize is that the people who arrived at eight in the morning and left at eight at night still worked a twelve-hour day. The people who were complaining had arrived at nine and were leaving at nine, but both groups had worked a total of twelve hours; they worked the same amount of time!

An even greater example comes from later in my career outside of public accounting when timecards weren't kept for billable hours to clients. Some people would arrive as early as seven in the morning and then leave promptly at five while taking lunch at their desk so that they could get home to have dinner with their families. Once again, I overheard several conversations, and the greatest extreme involved not just two people, but three who would arrive at ten o'clock in the morning and then stay until six in the evening, while taking an average lunch break of an hour to run errands. That's only seven hours total!

Once again, these three people were commenting on those who leave promptly at five and how they must not have any work ethic . . . except they were including several people in that statement who had actually worked a ten-hour day! Ten hours in total is more than seven, but to those who fall into this perception, it's easy to judge that which you do not know.

When clear objectives and measures of performance are used as the basis for rewards, especially in hiring decisions or in promotions, this will allow more people to know and feel that the decisions affecting their careers and work lives are fair and honest.

Positive

Reinforcement

If you want your garden to grow, you need to water your plants. If you want your plants to grow in an attractive pattern, you need to trim them strategically and make sure they're getting plenty of light so that they will grow as you desire instead of in a direction that you don't desire.

Positive reinforcement encourages repeated behavior. When you offer praise in response to something that was performed that you liked, you make people feel good about themselves and they will want to repeat it. Tell them what you like about what they have done and they will do it again. Suggest ways for them to do other parts better after having offered positive reinforcement over the whole, and they will want to incorporate those suggestions because they're not being offered as criticism and are allowing them to receive future praise and even more positive reinforcement.

No matter how many times a person has done something for you previously, it's always appropriate and welcome to thank them for doing it for you again. "Thank you" goes a long way.

If you offer positive reinforcement for something that someone has done, even if they have other things that they still need to do, you can make them happy enough to receive your next suggestion, which is really your desire. And if presented in exactly the right way, the person may even believe it was their original idea. For example, let's say that someone compiled an analysis for you and you like the direction they were going in; they included many of the things you'd expect and had wanted, but there was just one or two things missing that you'd really like to see in the report. Some would directly call out, "These parts can stay as they are, but you didn't complete these other pieces that we need in the report, so go back and add them and then share the final report with me."

A better approach would be this: "Wow, that's a great report. I really love the way you included these items; that's really going to help with my analysis and was very thoughtful. I especially like how you presented these two items before this third item over here because it makes it nice and easy for me to read. You know what, can we do this for X and Y too? If we could add X and Y to this report, this would be even more awesome. You really have something here! If we could add these items before so and so arrives, we could really impress them! How soon could you add them to the report?"

Now doesn't that sound better? A motivated person would

be very happy that their boss was so impressed with their report that they wanted more of it, that it wasn't a failure, that it actually lead to even greater desire for the performance. The boss liked it so much they wanted even more!

Now if the employee had heard the first statement, they'd be thinking about how they didn't meet their boss' expectations and they'd finish the report, but they wouldn't be very excited about it. It's just expected of them; there's nothing intrinsically rewarding for having done it, and they may even worry how it's going to reflect on their annual evaluation.

This is even a two-way street. The more you focus on confirming the self in others, the more they will feel inclined to do the same for you. Unlike negativity, this can turn into an upward spiral and not only will they feel good about coming into work, but you will feel the same when they reciprocate back with their smiles or their own appreciation of you as a leader and a manager.

All in all, you get a lot more out of people if you use positive reinforcement, and their morale will be much higher. They will enjoy working with you more because you make them feel good about themselves. This confirms the ego. They will be more likely to take the changes you've suggested and even come up with some suggestions of their own in the future to see if they can do even better. If they feel that their ego will be confirmed by performing work for you, they will want to perform it even more.

Relating to Others

We're not alone in this world, and it's a very fortunate thing. Without positive human contact, we become depressed, self-destructive, you name it. Humans are complex, but most of us are social creatures, even if we're shy. To return to the mission "to manage morale and motivate people," we need to try to understand someone if we're going to find out what uniquely motivates them.

Take a few minutes and imagine yourself having grown up as the other person grew up, having seen what they've seen and all of the experiences that have come together to shape them and their view of the world. Our perception forms our reality, and our reality is our world. Often when someone exhibits negativity, it's because of their own frustrations and fears. At least, that's one of the easier causes to overcome. If someone is negative to you, they rarely know who you really are, so just remember that and it will be much easier to disassociate their comments from your own sense of self worth.

Instead, ask yourself what's happening to them to cause them to be so full of negative emotion that they feel the need to unburden themselves on you. If you can find the cause or rerun in your mind what this other person has been through in their life, it may make it easier to address them.

Sometimes when people become offensive, they often believe that they are actually being defensive — defensive against a world that has mistreated them in their own mind. Real or imagined, events and ideas spark our emotions, both positive and negative, more than anything else. If we can find what is troubling them, we may be able to identify an easy way to calm them, or to let them know that their part of the world with you is safe, and whatever they've experienced before or believe they have experienced, isn't something that you're going to remind them of or make them repeat if they've felt pain.

But on the other side of the same coin, negativity is the fastest way to destroy relationships. If a person cannot be soothed easily, and refuses to play well with others, then they may be bringing down the rest of the team and causing much undeserved stress that will derail your efforts in motivating people and creating an environment of positive morale.

Eliminating
Negativity

In any group, there will be those who complain. Some people are just not happy unless they're unhappy . . . and even then they're not happy. You probably know the type of person that I'm talking about. They're usually the first to offer a negative opinion when new ideas are introduced. They usually complain vocally about their perception as to how someone or everyone is unfair to them. This type of person is a vocal pessimist, and they can do great harm to a company culture if not kept in check.

Vocal pessimists usually choose to complain to those who are not in a position to solve their problems. They want those they complain to validate their opinions. By receiving validation of their opinions, although negative, they feel better about feeling the way that they do. But it only encourages even more negative thoughts and complaints.

When they feel that their grievances haven't been validated by those they choose to complain to, they often become more upset, distant, or even confrontational. In the chapter on the Ego, we discussed why people want their feelings to be validated, except that what these people do not realize is that they are creating a negative culture.

A much more serious threat to morale and a positive work environment are those who are truly confrontational. These people often try to justify their actions by just saying that they are "direct" or "just being honest." But I haven't met anyone yet who uses this word to describe themselves who doesn't have frequent problems when working with people. The truth is, directness itself can be inappropriate in the wrong circumstance. Directness is confrontation.

Bad news is often best delivered in a soft and indirect (non-confrontational) manner. Voice tones are important and body language is important because it doesn't matter what you say if you are yelling. And what constitutes yelling isn't necessarily the volume level of the speaker; it's the tone and the perceived anger behind it! Anger or frustration in the speaker is noticed by the receiver. Habitually angry people usually require significant life-altering experiences, and even after these significant experiences, they must choose to view the world in a new light and change for the better rather than to become even more bitter.

I'm sure you know what I mean when I just leave this description as "mean people".

We all experience frustration at times. Sometimes something we've been working on just fell apart, or we've been the subject of criticism ourselves, and in these cases it can often seem tempting to lash out at someone who causes you additional challenge or frustration, or needs your time to answer a question, but you have so little time to spare that it upsets you. But don't do it! At times, it can seem like unleashing your anger on someone will allow you to release it and make you feel better . . . but if you relate well to others and value a part of yourself in the way that others think about you, it will only give you a cause of regret when you see the hurt or tears on the other person's face, or feel their retaliation in anger against you.

At times it can be tempting to tell someone who misunderstood you, "Can't you get that through your thick skull?" or "I expected more from you," or something like that. But it's not positive.

Beyond the factual statement of work tasks to perform, anything that is said with the intention of communicating or transferring anger will be seen as an insult. If they feel insulted by you, do you really expect them to give you all that they have to give?

Before you choose the message you are about to communicate to someone, remember what you want them to do with that information, and act accordingly so that your message will have the desired effect. In most cases, you'll be pleasantly surprised with the results.

When giving constructive criticism, stick to the facts. Most people will feel bad enough that they're being told their first attempt wasn't perfect. We all want to be perfect, but if you at least allow them to keep their sense of self, they will want to fix it because they will want to please you and know that you will say, "thank you" and "good job" and generally reinforce their feeling of self worth.

And actions speak just as loudly as words. A genuine smile and lightheartedness can lighten the impact of a statement, but still communicate what you have to say; while a very stern statement with a scowl, frown, or stare, is often perceived as anger in the speaker, just like the tone of voice. A truly fake smile (think of the Grinch who stole Christmas) isn't positive either, so remember that the best way to let people know they can trust you is to be genuine AND open with your welcoming body language.

Be aware of your body language; crossed arms are a sign of being closed off and defensive. A defensive stance can turn into an offensive one quickly, and observant people will pick up on that. For example, in certain cultures it's polite to keep your hands in your lap when sitting at the dinner table, but in other cultures it's considered suspicious. And in gambling circles it can be seen as threatening (is that person going to pull a weapon on me and take my money because they're angry about having lost money in a card game?). Often just keeping good posture and eye contact with a smile is enough to show the other person that you are happy and not annoyed to see them. Refusing to turn to see them, not smiling, and forgetting to say "hello" or "goodnight," on the other hand, can make the other person believe you're not feeling friendly. To return to the concept of making work fun, we all want to feel that we are working among friends.

Once you've made an insult, it's extremely hard to regain that person's trust. They will not want to open themselves up to you and risk having their sense of self become attacked again. Humans and animals alike are predisposed to run from their fears, or attack when cornered. If you've knowingly hurt someone's feelings, the only way to regain their respect is to start with an apology.

Not all the compliments in the world can erase an insult. You can say a hundred good things about a person and then say "but" and say something negative, and they will hang onto that one negative thing. It can be enough to reduce their motivation to please you.

Returning to the topic of vocal pessimists, propagating negative thoughts without offering a solution can turn into a spiral, or even create its own negative culture in that the members who choose to become a part of this clique have nothing to share unless they are sharing negative thoughts. They want to be heard and they want the company of others, and if others give into them, then the group that is founded on negativity alone cannot exist without it. Eventually, they create their own negativity and become a consistent problem if you're trying to raise the morale of those around you.

The best way to diffuse vocal pessimists is to talk to them directly and to listen to them once. If their concerns are truly not productive or perhaps not remotely valid, acknowledge that you have listened, but tell them immediately that you expect them to offer a solution rather than a complaint. If they cannot offer a reasonable solution themselves, or are not willing to consider a solution proposed by you in an attempt to appease them, then the best thing you can really do is to issue them a warning. Put it into writing, perhaps even create a contract, or specify that their continued employment is contingent upon their successful completion of a course chosen by you. (I prefer Dale Carnegie courses because of the results that I have seen).

If they're willing to make the inner changes necessary to not destroy the company culture, then they may be salvageable; but if they've been given an honest chance and refuse to change, then they've made the decision to stick with their addiction to negativity, and much like an addition to drugs, there really is no place for this in the workplace. It's as dangerous and harmful to allow it to continue as it would be to let a drunken forklift driver lift pallets with bystanders around them.

Just like Dorothy in the Wizard of OZ was afraid to enter

the woods due to "lions, tigers, and bears," your positive people will feel the same apprehension when they enter the workplace if they anticipate vocal pessimists and "mean" people.

I like to believe that anyone can change, and that everyone wants to be the best that they can be, and to be happy. But there are plenty of happy people in the workplace and you can't let a vocal pessimist or "mean" person destroy the company's morale if all attempts have been made to correct the problem and they are unwilling to cooperate.

If they're truly unhappy, then set them free to find their own happiness; this could be the best thing for them although they may not see it immediately. Each person deserves to be happy, and if they can't be happy here, they really need to search their inner self to find what it is that they could do that would make them happy, because happiness is a choice. Happiness isn't a destination that you arrive at; it's a method of traveling by.

Even if you're afraid of losing the technical expertise of the people who are "mean" or who are repeated vocal pessimists, it's your place to protect those who rely on you. Ask not who you are cutting, ask who you are allowing to stay, because if you don't remove negativity from the workplace, your best people will move on.

You may experience the cost of turnover, but anyone can be replaced if technical knowledge is all that they have to offer. The ability to learn and exposure to the material is all that's required to get someone with a similar skill set to that same level of technical knowledge that's required to do the job.

Individual Technical
Failures

Every so often someone's set of
skills doesn't match the job and try
as they may with the best of
intentions, they may not have the

learning style to reach the knowledge level required of the specific job. This is especially hard when the person has a lot of enthusiasm and has the level of morale that you wish to maintain or create for your team. This doesn't mean that they're not worth something; they may be very good at something else other than what they've been assigned to.

Your job in this situation is to help them find their strengths and to counsel them into sharpening those strengths so that they can reach the highest level of competency at what they do best, even if this isn't with your company.

We all feel good when we're doing something that we know we're good at. The person may be perfect for another position within the same company, and they could help to build relationships between departments by moving into another role. Or, if there is a sales component to the job, this person could be the key to future business you may receive with their next employer. Try to help them, and to lead them into their own honest answer.

Often they will admit that the position they are trying to perform isn't what they do well. If they still aren't looking to make a change after you've counseled them at first, then give them more guidance as to where they should be looking. Let them think well of you. You should have their best interests in mind and you're not trying to hurt them; you're mentoring them into the best that they can be.

In this day and age, companies seem more likely to lay off groups of workers due to economic problems than to counsel individual workers who are failing at the tasks they've been assigned.

But first, make sure you give them every opportunity to succeed, and every opportunity to learn the job at hand. Some jobs can take a year or more before the average person knows all of the ins and outs, and at least a month or so before they start to add value and can operate in your system.

This section certainly isn't for employees who are just new to the job; this is for those who you no longer have reasonable hope of training to perform the function that you need performed.

Final Thoughts

We spend an incredible amount of our waking hours at work, and most of us derive something of our self-esteem from the work that we do. If you can manage your workplace morale and make it a happy place for people to come to work, you will have far more to look forward to every day. You will be remembered by those you've worked with as being a fair and likable person. You'll find that you have friends wherever you go. Each life time is finite, so let's make the best of it and enjoy as much of it as we can.